Unlocking God's Favor

Bernice Brown Gregory

Write the vision make it plain. Habakkuk 2:2

1ˢᵗ Edition Copyright© 2015

Unlocking God's Favor – by Bernice Brown Gregory

Library of Congress Cataloging in Publication Data

Published by, Chloe Arts and Publishing, LLC

P.O. Box 26054

St. Louis Park, MN 55426

Graphic: Bernice Brown Gregory

Edited: Chloe Staff

ISBN: 978-0-692-59319-6

Printed and bound in the United States of America

Dedication

To my loving husband Percelle, who is always by my side and supports me to heaven's end. Darling, I love you dearly.

To our son James, who God gifted to us, who we will always cherish and love.

To my mom, Ella Mae Brown, Sr., who is my rock who taught me to pray, love the Lord and the reason I am a born again Christian today. Mom, I love you dearly.

To my daddy, Clifford James Brown, Sr. and my mother-in-love, Wilma Prince Gregory, while, on earth they stuck by me, loved me and supported me in all my endeavors. I will forever be eternally grateful for the both of you. R.I.P. Daddy and Mom Wilma.

Forward

Unlocking God's Favor simplifies how to open treasures He has placed in your life. It will take you on a journey of learning how to unlock His favor in the areas you need His favor the most.

As you read, each chapter watch how they allow you to gain more knowledge and a new level of understanding of His will for your life.

After watching Bernice spend hours allowing God to give her insight for readers to gain His favor, I believe you will not be disappointed with what God has given her for your benefit.

I am very proud to be her husband, and grateful she is an anointed vessel that allows God to use her in every area of her and our lives because it was that anointing that rescued me from a world of darkness.

I am so honored she said, yes, when I asked her to marry me. Be blessed, and enjoy Unlocking God's Favor!

Dr. Percelle G. Gregory

Introduction

Unlocking God's Favor was written with the intention of giving you some insight as to how I was able to gain God's Favor through prayer, faith, and His written word. God requires us to trust Him and believe that His word will be done just the way He said it would. I like how it says in Titus 1:2, In hope of eternal life, which God, that cannot lie, promised before the world began. It is so good to know that we have an expected end because our Heavenly Father does not lie and even greater than that cannot lie.

There is a song that goes "I was sinking deep in sin, far from the peaceful shores, very deeply stained within, sinking to rise no more, but the Master of the sea heard my despairing cry and from the waters lifted me now safe am I." This describes how my life was heading until I gave it over to the Lord. .

While reading Unlocking God's Favor, you will find a brief synopsis of how I was able to unlock God's favor, which you will find in the chapters such as Favor through Finances, Obedience, Single, Married, Divorce, and Remarried.

I am so excited about sharing this information with you and pray it will help direct you in the right direction to gain His favor in the areas you may need it. Are you ready?

Let's go!

Table of Contents

Chapter I
Unlocking God's Favor
When Doing His Will
Seems Unfavorable

Merriam Webster defines "favor" as a friendly regard shown toward another especially by a superior. Well, no one is any more superior to God. I wanted to start out by giving a definition of "favor" to explain how writing this book came about.

One night I was awakened by a still small voice impressing me to begin writing about ways to unlock His favor. I knew in my heart that God wants us all to be free from sin, fear, and bondage. He also wants us to be able to walk in the newness of Him after gaining knowledge and wisdom in how to unlock His favor. All of which will allow us to become very healthy, very wealthy and very wise. God speaks through His written word, in 3 John 1:2, He says, "Beloved, I wish above all that you may prosper and be in good health even as your soul prospers."

One may ask, how I can begin *Unlocking God's Favor?* One answer would be through prayer. The Holy Bible says in I Thessalonians 5:17, to "pray without ceasing."

**Unlocking God's Favor
When Doing His Will
Seems Unfavorable**

I found this scripture to be true as it plays a very significant part in my daily walk with the Lord.

In 2004, the Lord placed a desire in my heart to produce a gospel music CD project. I knew it was Him because personally I had no desire to do a music project. It was birthed when my Aunt Mamie, asked me to tape myself singing some songs and send them for her personal listening. But this was a stepping stone, unbeknownst to me, to my producing a full recording. God really does work in mysterious ways.

After being commissioned for this project, I remember saying to myself, "Oh that will be easy." My reasoning was because I sing, I felt all I had to do was push a record button and start singing. But I found out what God had planned was much larger than that. He wanted me to do a full-fledged recording. And I did not have a clue, other than what I have seen on TV, how to go about it to complete the project.

**Unlocking God's Favor
When Doing His Will
Seems Unfavorable**

At first, I tried doing it my way, and it was time-consuming and even at times painful. I had to learn from experience that the only way to do this, was to do it God's way and not my way. You see, I came from a ministry that taught us to believe in the power of God. But I must admit, even though I said I believed, my actions were doing otherwise. I had begun to step out on my own and found myself running into stumbling block after stumbling block. I did not have a clue as to how to produce a gospel CD neither was I knowledgeable about the gospel music industry.

After running into those stumbling blocks (mistakes), I found myself questioning God, "Where are you?" or as we say in church "Where Art Thou?" But honestly God in His loving and kind way forgave me and gave me the instructions I needed to steer me in the direction to get the job done. One of those instructions was to have one hour of prayer every evening. I thought for sure he meant for me to have this prayer time on my own in the convenience of my home.

Unlocking God's Favor
When Doing His Will
Seems Unfavorable

Later, I found it was for me to go to the church and pray in the sanctuary during this hour of prayer. At that time, I did not understand why, but after doing so, I found there were others who had a desire to pray at church in the evening. It was their desire to unlock God's favor, when doing His will seemed unfavorable; what an encouragement. Before others had started coming, I felt it was just me, but the Lord reminded me He has a host of angels worshiping him and other intercessors around the world praying, so I decided to stop complaining and join in with them.

While walking in obedience to God by leading the evening prayer, I began to experience the unlocking of God's favor. It came through ways opening up for us to complete the project within months versus years that it could have taken had I continued to do it my way. "It pays to do it God's way."

**Unlocking God's Favor
When Doing His Will
Seems Unfavorable**

I found out that doing it His way was through fasting and praying. Once you get the answer from Him, hold Him accountable to His word as it says in Isaiah 55:6, Seek the Lord while He may be found and call upon Him while He is near. Another verse I keep close to my heart while working on the CD project is found in Philippians 4:13, I can do all things through Christ that strengthens me; we apply this verse to our everyday lives. You can bank on the Word of God working in your favor because Ephesians 3:20 says, He can do exceeding and abundantly above all we can ask or think, according to the power that worketh in us. This is what we stood on, and it built our faith to the point God's favor was unlocked (revealed). The people we needed to meet and things we needed to complete the assignment began to come our way. We received financial support, songwriters, producers, a full band, background singers, radio promoters, newspaper and magazine editors who did feature articles to support what we were doing.

**Unlocking God's Favor
When Doing His Will
Seems Unfavorable**

I have to tell you, I was so blessed to write some of the songs on the project. I was not aware I had that talent on the inside of me, and it was very exciting to see that take place in my life. You may ask why did this happen? It was because I finally got in line with what He wanted and not what I wanted, and today I can proudly say the title of my first CD project by way of unlocking God's favor was birthed and titled: ***God's Been Good to Me.***

This completed project is a prime example of *Unlocking God's Favor, When Doing His Will Seems Unfavorable.*

Scripture References:

II Chronicles 22:19 (AMP), Now set your mind and heart to seek the Lord your God. Arise and build the sanctuary of the Lord God, So that the Ark of Covenant of the Lord and the holy vessels of God may be brought into the house built on the Name and renown of the Lord.

**Unlocking God's Favor
When Doing His Will
Seems Unfavorable**

Jeremiah 29:11-13 (NIV), For I know the plans I have for you, "declares the Lord," plans to prosper you and not to harm you, plans to give you hope and a future. Then you will call on me and come and pray to me, and I will listen to you. You will seek me and find me when you seek me with your heart.

Matthew 7:7 (NIV), Ask and it will be given to you; seek and you will find; knock and the door will be opened to you.

Deuteronomy 4:29 (NIV), But if from there you seek the Lord your God, you will find him if you seek him with all your heart and with all your soul.

I Chronicles 16:11 (NAS), Seek the Lord and His Strength, Seek His face continually.

Chapter II
Unlocking God's Favor
For Healing

Whenever I share my testimony of being healed from diabetes, I always tell them my motto is, "I am too busy to be sick and too cute to be cut on." I chose to live my life as a healed woman of God and be what He wants me to be, which is fully healthy, very wealthy and very wise. It is my desire to encourage you, if you need to unlock God's favor for healing, you must do what it takes to change your negative situation and then God will step in and do the rest.

A key scripture to stand on is Philippians 4:13 (KJV), I can do all things through Christ which strengtheneth me. My personal interpretation of this verse is, I MUST DO, BEFORE HE WILL STRENGTHEN ME TO DO WHAT I NEED TO DO, TO CHANGE MY SITUATION. Please note, if you do it God's way by believing in His word and apply it to your daily life, you can and will be healed from anything.

**Unlocking God's Favor
For Healing**

There are benefits from having a relationship with Christ, and one is healing. Therefore, if you are in need of healing why not trust God and receive your healing. If it worked for me, it will work for anyone.

Scripture References:

I Peter 2:21 (KJV), For even hereunto were ye called: because Christ also suffered for us, leaving us an example, that ye should follow his steps.

Isaiah 53:5, But he was wounded for our transgressions, he was bruised for our iniquities; the chastisement of our peace was upon him; and with his stripes we are healed.

Psalms 103:2-3, Bless the Lord, O my soul, and forget not all his benefits. Who forgives all thine iniquities; who healeth all thy diseases.

**Unlocking God's Favor
For Healing**

While believing God for healing after being diagnosed by the doctor with diabetes, one might want to know who to go to for prayer to get healed. Sadly, everyone does not know how to pray by faith and get the results from God they need. In this chapter, I speak on how I was able to unlock God's favor for healing for what I was facing. I praise God for my husband and my pastors who I love dearly. They stood by me during this trying time in my life. I received a call from my doctor, that I can remember like it was yesterday; it seemed like a call from hell. He said, Ms. Gregory, you have Type 2, Diabetes. I can honestly say that because I knew what God's Word said about healing, I made up my mind right away, I was not going to accept the diagnosis. After stating the results of the lab report, I explained to him what the Word of God said "the fact may be Type 2, Diabetes, but the truth was stated in I Peter 2:24, BY HIS STRIPES WE WERE HEALED.

**Unlocking God's Favor
For Healing**

So the Word of the Lord was the only diagnosis I was going to accept. Some may say I am crazy to believe God's word over the medical report, but they are not walking in my shoes, and I know for a fact that doctor reports can change for the better and praise God, mine did. Starting the process of being healed, came through studying the word of God, fasting, praying, and believing Him for my healing. In addition to all that was happening at the time of the diagnosis, I was weighing 314 pounds that I knew was too much weight for a body frame of 5'3." So to get what I needed from God, I had to unlock His favor for healing. I had to change my eating habits, exercise (yes, exercise) for at least 30 minutes a day and due to what I was facing, I chose to exercise 7 days a week. At that time, it was my decision to take it one day at a time, and here it is now over ten years. I must add, the bonus from the weight loss was I went down from a size 28 to a size 16. Again, I praise God because I can now be healthy and diabetes free.

**Unlocking God's Favor
For Healing**

Scripture References:

Jeremiah 30:17 (KJV), For I will restore health unto thee, and I will heal thee of thy wounds, saith the Lord; because they called thee an Outcast, saying, this is Zion, whom no man seeketh after.

James 5:14-16 (KJV), Is any sick among you? Let him call for the elders of the church; and let them pray over him, anointing him with oil in the name of the Lord: And the prayer of faith shall save the sick, and the Lord shall raise him up; and if he has committed sins, they shall be forgiven him. Confess [your] faults one to another, and pray one for another, that ye may be healed. The effectual fervent prayer of a righteous man availeth much.

3 John 1:2 (KJV), Beloved, I wish above all things that thou mayest prosper and be in health, even as thy soul prospereth

Chapter III
Unlocking God's Favor
For Deliverance From Fear

About 40 years ago, I lived my life in fear. I was afraid to drive for fearing of being in a car accident, afraid of flying due to the plane possibly crashing, afraid of going on a cruise because I watched the Titanic, afraid of riding a train, or a bus it might crash. It didn't matter what form of transportation it was, I was afraid to the point I stayed in the house most of the time and all I would do was eat and sleep, which played a great deal in my overweight situation.

I have to admit this part of my life was totally due to not praying and staying in communication with God. I needed to build a prayer life and do as it says in I Thessalonians 5:17, Pray without ceasing. A funny thing about life is we are taught things in our childhood that could make us or break us later on in life. As a child, one of the positive things I was taught was *Prayer is the Key to the Kingdom, and Faith Unlocks the Door.* This is what the gist of the book you are now reading is based on, being told about prayer being the Key to the Kingdom.

**Unlocking God's Favor
For Deliverance From Fear**

As an adult, I have come to realize it is a true fact that by praying and believing the Word of God, it has kept me free from being bound by fear. Fear, to the point I would not leave the house to travel to many parts of the world, but now I have an assurance he is protecting me, and I am not afraid to drive. It just might have a little bit to do with God blessings us with a new Mercedes Benz, so you know "Sister Girl" is not afraid to drive that. Please note, MY GOD IS FAITHFUL! Being delivered from fear allowed me to accomplish doing a CD project because when doing something of that magnitude there were a lot of major business decisions to be made in a snap without guessing or possibly making wrong decisions because if we had they would have been very costly. Therefore, there was no room fear.

My husband and I both learned to be confident and know as the scripture states in Philippians 4:13, I can do all things through Christ that strengthens me. If there is any task you are facing that seems hard or impossible, try trusting God and applying His Word to your daily living, it will help to make it easier for you to live your life to its fullest. Also, you will be able to live a life free from fear. Fear is an enemy, but trusting God will allow you to conquer that enemy. "Trust God."

**Unlocking God's Favor
For Deliverance From Fear**

Scripture References:

Hebrews 13:6 (KJV), So that we may boldly say. The Lord is my helper, and I will not fear what man shall do unto me.

Proverbs 14:26 (KJV), In the fear of the Lord is strong confidence: and his children shall have a place of refuge.

Philippians 4:6-7 (KJV), Be careful for nothing; but in everything by prayer and supplication with thanksgiving let your request be made known unto God. And the peace of God, which passeth all understanding, shall keep your hearts and minds through Christ Jesus.

Psalms 91:5-6 (KJV), Thou shall not be afraid for the terror by night; nor for the arrow that flieth by day; Nor for the pestilence that walketh in darkness; nor for the destruction that wasteth at noonday.

Psalms 91:7, A thousand shall fall at thy side, and ten thousand at thy right hand; but it shall not come nigh thee.

**Unlocking God's Favor
For Deliverance From Fear**

Scripture References:

II Timothy 1:7 (KJV), For God hath not given us the spirit of fear, but of power, and of love and of a sound mind.

Jeremiah 42:6 (KJV), Whether it be good, or whether it be evil, we will obey the voice of the LORD our God, to whom we send thee; that it may be well with us, when we obey the voice of the LORD our God

I Samuel 15:22 KJV), And Samuel said, Hath the LORD as great delight in burnt offerings and sacrifices, as in obeying the voice of the LORD? Behold, to obey is better than sacrifice, and to hearken than the fat of rams.

Proverbs 3: 5-6 (KJV), Trust in the LORD with all thine heart; and lean not unto thine own understanding.6In all thy ways acknowledge him, and he shall direct thy paths

Jeremiah 17:14, Heal me, O LORD, and I shall be healed; save me, and I shall be saved: for thou [art] my praise

**Unlocking God's Favor
For Deliverance From Fear**

Scripture References:

3 John 1:2, Beloved, I wish above all things that thou mayest prosper and be in health, even as thy soul prospereth

Proverbs 17:22, A merry heart doeth good [like] a medicine: but a broken spirit drieth the bones.

Matthew 10:1, When he had called unto [him] his twelve disciples, he gave them power [against] unclean spirits, to cast them out, and to heal all manner of sickness and all manner of disease.

Psalms 127:3, Lo, children [are] an heritage of the LORD: [and] the fruit of the womb [is his] reward.

I Peter 2:24, Who his own self bare our sins in his own body on the tree that we, being dead to sins, should live unto righteousness: by whose stripes ye were healed.

Jeremiah 33:6, Behold, I will bring it health and cure, and I will cure them, and will reveal unto them the abundance of peace and truth.

**Unlocking God's Favor
For Deliverance From Fear**

Scripture References:

Isaiah 53:5, He [was] wounded for our transgressions, [he was] bruised for our iniquities: the chastisement of our peace [was] upon him; and with his stripes we are healed.

Matthew 10:8, Heal the sick, cleanse the lepers, raise the dead, cast out devils: freely ye have received, freely give.

Deuteronomy 7:15, And the LORD will take away from thee all sickness, and will put none of the evil diseases of Egypt, which thou knowest, upon thee; but will lay them upon all [them] that hate thee.

Chapter IV
Unlocking God's Favor
For Wisdom

To unlock God's favor for wisdom, I found myself reading and studying the book of Proverbs. Studying, I gained so much knowledge and wisdom that still helps me in my everyday life. I learned that God's wisdom is a gift from him that everyone does not possess.

God created wisdom from the beginning of time. His wisdom will teach you how to be quiet when you want to speak (to avoid saying the wrong thing and making the situation worse), pray when you want to fight, and sing when you want to give up. I am so glad I learned to apply the principle of listening to God (who can speak to your spouse, parents, children, or others). He will instruct you on how to do, when to do, and what to do. God made man and has total insight on how to deal with man.

It pays to pray and hear from the Lord, because it will get you further ahead in life when you do so.

Unlocking God's Favor
For Wisdom

There were many times I wanted to take matters into my own hands, especially when it came down to raising my son and having grandchildren. I have learned whenever it is a negative situation concerning them, and I chose to use wisdom, turning the negative situation over to Jesus, because He can work the situation out and turn it into a positive one.

Like the Bible instructs us, "What the enemy (Satan) meant for evil, God turned it around for the good," and also like I heard a preacher say, "It pays to follow Jesus." Let the church say, Amen!

I learned from my own experiences that wisdom will eliminate hurt feelings if you don't allow them to dictate to you. Wisdom will show you how to treat life's let downs and help you to have a positive attitude that things will turn around for the good. I like to look at it like this, "The sun will shine in the morning."

Unlocking God's Favor
For Wisdom

God's wisdom will give you ways to overlook hurt from family members, close friends, co-workers, and forgive them. In other words, forget the offense and move forward. I know that I have offended others that have forgiven me, and released me. So why not do to them what you would want in return. "Do unto others as you would have them do unto you." Through this, I can honestly pray, "Lord, forgive us our trespasses as we forgive those who trespass against us."

It is very important to forgive because unforgiveness can lead you to think evil towards others, and from there it can escalate into something you never thought could happen, all because you allowed yourself by your lack of forgiveness to be opened up to Satan's evil devices.

All in all, pray for God's wisdom, which leads you into all truth to know how to handle life on a daily basis.

**Unlocking God's Favor
For Wisdom**

If you do not know how to gain wisdom from God, it is found in James 1:5, if any man lack wisdom, let him ask of God and he will give it liberally. I absolutely love this verse because not only does He give it to us, but He gives it liberally (in abundance). So, pray for wisdom and by faith you will unlock God's favor for wisdom.

Scripture References:

Proverbs 2:2, 6, 10 (KJV), So that thou incline thine ear unto wisdom, and apply thine heart to understanding; For the LORD giveth wisdom: out of his mouth cometh knowledge and understanding. When wisdom entereth into thine heart and knowledge is pleasant unto thy soul;

James 1:5, If any of you lack wisdom, let him ask of God, that giveth to all [men] liberally, and upbraideth not; and it shall be given him

**Unlocking God's Favor
For Wisdom**

Scripture References:

Ephesians 5:15-17, See then that ye walk circumspectly, not as fools, but as wise

James 3:17, But the wisdom that is from above is first pure, then , gentle, [and] easy to be entreated, full of mercy and good fruits, without partiality, and without hypocrisy.

Proverbs 3:13, Happy [is] the man [that] findeth wisdom, and the man [that] getteth understanding.

Proverbs 10:23, [It is] as sport to a fool to do mischief: but a man of understanding hath wisdom.

Proverbs 12:15, The way of a fool [is] right in his own eyes: but he that hearkeneth unto counsel [is] wise.

Proverbs 18:5, The heart of the prudent getteth knowledge; and the ear of the wise seeketh knowledge.

**Unlocking God's Favor
For Wisdom**

Scripture References:

Colossians 3:16, Let the word of Christ dwell in you richly in all wisdom; teaching and admonishing one another in psalms and hymns and spiritual songs, singing with grace in your hearts to the Lord.

Proverbs 17:27, He that hath knowledge spareth his words: [and] a man of understanding is of an excellent spirit.

Proverbs 19:20, Hear counsel, and receive instruction, that thou mayest be wise in thy latter end.

Ecclesiastes 8:1, Who [is] as the wise [man]? and who knoweth the interpretation of a thing? a man's wisdom maketh his face to shine, and the boldness of his face shall be changed.

Psalms 121:1-2, I will lift up mine eyes unto the hills, from whence cometh my help. My help cometh from the LORD, which made heaven and earth.

Chapter V
Unlocking God's Favor
Through Worship

In worshiping God, you can unlock His favor. Worshiping him with a pure heart allows you to enter into the heart of God and be led by Him in every aspect of your life. Some believe praising God is the same as worshiping God. But the truth of the matter is praise is when you are praising Him along with others, but when you worship God, you are in one on one communication with Him.

I was in a situation of dealing with unforgiveness towards a family member. I don't know about you, but forgiving family can be a hard thing to do, at least at the time it was for me. Through worshiping God, the answer came, and that was to get spiritual counseling on how to deal with the situation.

During this time, I was dealing with some health issues and in the counseling sessions I was encouraged to get myself checked out by a physician, and also to check my spiritual heart to make sure there was no unforgiveness towards anyone. I learned that unforgiveness can turn into bitterness, and that the Bible teaches that bitterness is as rottenness to the bones. After learning that I let go of the unforgiveness and guess what, I have not had that health issue ever again.

Unlocking God's Favor Through Worship

The Bible states for us not to offer God any heathen worship; I don't have time for my worship not to be true worship unto. A very important part of my life is to give God true worship, glory and honor. God is FAITHFUL, and He is worthy to be praised, so we must worship Him in spirit and in truth.

There are many benefits in worshiping God; they include joy, peace, happiness, direction, and comfort along with many others. God is a loving God, and you will experience His love when you learn to worship Him. Worshiping feels like it is just you and Him with no interruptions. You can tell Him how you feel and what you are feeling without worrying about Him judging you. Actually, He already knows how you feel and His mercy allows you to express your true feelings. If you are wrong, His love corrects you and gets you back on course. Now isn't that good to know?

Unlocking God's Favor Through Worship

Many times as humans, we seem to be afraid to express our love to God, but that is what He desires of us. Psalm 22:3 says, "But thou are holy, O thou that inhabitest the praises of Israel." He loves it when we worship Him because He already loves us to the point he gave us his ultimate sacrifice and that was His only son Jesus. I'm not sure how many people would be willing to sacrifice their only child to save humanity.

While working on the CD music project, I learned what it meant to worship God in spirit and in truth. Doing so, I gained a greater relationship with Him. He taught me how to hear and understand His voice. For me, it is a small whisper that directs me in the area that I need it. His voice allowed me to finish the project he assigned me to.

Unlocking God's Favor
Through Worship

Submitting to His will, knowing His voice and His timing, everything that seemed wrong at the time of working on the project became right. I learned through this project that people you think are will help you, because they are in a position to help, may not necessarily be the ones God has assigned to do so. It is often the ones you least expect. You may ask, why is that? Well, I asked God for that answer, and I found out God wants to get all the Glory. We as people when we can do something or know someone that can do it for us, we seem to take credit or give the credit to the person that helped us, and not to God, who made it all possible.

Real worshipers can attest that there is nothing like worshiping God Almighty. To be honest, you really can't explain it you have to experience it on your own.

In ending this, I would like to encourage you to learn or continue to give God true worship because as I said earlier, there are benefits when it comes to worshiping God in Spirit and Truth.

Unlocking God's Favor Through Worship

Scripture References:

Samuel 15:25, Now therefore, I pray thee, pardon my sin, and turn again with me, that I may worship the Lord

2Kings 17:36, But the Lord, who brought you up out of the land of Egypt with great power and a stretched out arm, him shall ye fear, and him shall ye worship, and to him shall ye do sacrifice.

Psalms 8:10, Lord, our Lord, how majestic is your name in all the earth! You have set your glory above the heavens.

Psalms 29:2, Ascribe to the Lord the glory due to his name; worship the LORD in splendor of Holiness.

Ephesians 5:19, Speaking to yourselves in psalms and hymns and spiritual songs, singing and making melody in your heart to the Lord;

**Unlocking God's Favor
Through Worship**

Scripture References:

1 John 1:3, That which we have seen and heard declare we unto you, that ye also may have fellowship with us: and truly our fellowship [is] with the Father, and with his Son Jesus Christ.

Hebrews 13:15, by him therefore let us offer the sacrifice of praise to God continually, that is, the fruit of [our] lips giving thanks to his name.

Romans 12:1, I beseech you therefore, brethren, by the mercies of God, that ye present your bodies a living sacrifice, holy, acceptable unto God, [which is] your reasonable service.

John 4:23, But the hour cometh, and now is, when the true worshippers shall worship the Father in spirit and in truth: for the Father seeketh such to worship him.

Colossians 3:16, Let the word of Christ dwell in you richly in all wisdom; teaching and admonishing one another in psalms and hymns and spiritual songs, singing with grace in your hearts to the Lord.

Matthew 16:24, Then said Jesus unto his disciples, If any [man] will come after me, let him deny himself, and take up his cross, and follow me.

Chapter VI
Unlocking God's Favor
Through Obedience

Galatians 5:7-8, Ye did run well, who did hinder you that ye should not obey the truth? I like how the New Living translation states it, "You were getting along doing well, who has interfered with you, to hold you back from following the truth." It is important to know that respecting those that are in authority can only give you access to the greater things you desire in life. In unlocking God's favor through respecting others, He will give you enough knowledge to know that respect can get you to the top versus being at the bottom. There is a quote that my pastor uses regarding obedience and respecting others, and that is "Your attitude determines your altitude."

I can remember when I was a child, we always got more from our parents when we were obedient, than when we tried to do things our own way; it works the same way with God. I know "obedient" seems to be a strong word when you're talking about obeying others, but it is just another way of respect to a greater degree.

Unlocking God's Favor
Through Obedience

The same goes with our Lord and Savior Jesus Christ when we learn to trust Him and obey his written Word (the Bible) we can only get ahead and unlock His favor. I once heard a preacher say, "Favor ain't fair, " which in short, means, others may be at the head of the line, but God's favor will put you at the head of the line when in reality, you were at the back of the line. "Won't He Do It?"

Be encouraged to be obedient when you are facing challenging situations and you find yourself wanting to do the opposite. Trust God and you will find out for sure, "obedience is better than sacrifice."

Scripture References:

Deuteronomy 28:1(NIV), If you fully obey the Lord your God and carefully follow all his commands I give you today, the Lord your God will set you high above all the nations on earth.

James 1:22 (NIV), Do not merely listen to the word, and so deceive yourselves. Do what it says.

Proverbs 10:17 (NIV), Whoever heeds discipline shows the way to life, but whoever ignores correction leads others astray.

Unlocking God's Favor
Through Obedience

Scripture References:

I Samuel 15:22 (NIV), But Samuel replied; "Does the Lord delight in burnt offerings and sacrifices, as much as in obeying the Lord? To obey is better than sacrifice, and to heed is better than the fat of rams.

Deuteronomy 5:33 (NIV), Walk in obedience to all that the Lord your God has commanded you, so that you may live and prosper and prolong your days in the land that you will possess.

Romans 1:5 (AMP), It is through Him that we have received grace (God's unmerited favor) and [our] apostleship to promote obedience to the faith and make disciples for His name's sake among all the   nations

Chapter VII
Unlocking God's Favor, Single, Married, Divorced, Remarried

Single

You know single life was not that favorable for me. It started out great. I gave me life to the Lord at the age of 13, and I really was excited about being saved until I let the later part of my teens get the best of me by not continuing to walk with the Lord. I found myself in a life that I was not proud of. And after that I felt I really would be happy if I found a husband and everything would be peaches and cream. Boy, oh boy, was I wrong.

I can honestly say I have been on all sides of the fence, singled, married, divorced and now remarried. After graduating from high school and moving on to college, one of the professors asked what we wanted to get out of college and when it was my turn, my answer was "to get a husband" even though people laughed I was serious.

**Unlocking God's Favor,
Single, Married, Divorced,
Remarried**

\

Married

Like I said after wanting so desperately to be married, I did meet and marry my husband during my college years. We only knew each other for five months, but that did not stop me from accepting his marriage proposal. I have to let you know, not only did I not seek the Lord about it, but I didn't even listen to my parents who were against the marriage. He had just graduated from school, and he was three years younger than me. Right, there was the downfall from the very beginning.

I must tell you my mother was and is a praying woman, and her response after meeting him was, "I wish you could see him through my eyes." But, oh no, he was the one, and I was not going to change my mind. So the marriage was on. I had decided that I was in love, and this was the man of my dreams and I was not going to let anyone talk me out of my decision.

**Unlocking God's Favor,
Single, Married, Divorced,
Remarried**

I knew the path I was going down, because of engaging in pre-marital activity, I needed to be married. At least that is what I thought I had to do if I was going to remain a Christian. I based it on I Corinthians 7:8-9 (KJV), "I say therefore to the unmarried and widows, it is good for them if they abide even as I. But if they cannot contain, let them marry: for it is better to marry than to burn." But in all actuality, what I needed to do was to say no to my flesh and be obedient to God.

I say it was my heart telling me this was my dream man, but it really was my head. I found out after stepping out on my own, my dream man turned into a nightmare. I can't blame it all on him because I was not perfect and we both should not have gotten married, at least not to each other, because frankly, neither one of us was ready at the time. The rest of this story will be in my next book (smile). Moving right along.

**Unlocking God's Favor,
Single, Married, Divorced,
Remarried**

Divorced

After the breakdown of the marriage really felt like a failure but was willing to stay in the relationship because I took my marriage vows very seriously, and I had married with the intention of staying married "until death due do us part." After all that went down, I sadly learned that it was never his intention of being married to me for the rest of his life.

To me, divorce was not an option but I must admit it was the best thing because the relationship had turned to be mentally abusive and was heading towards physical abuse on my end because I was a fighter before Christ. Do you want to know what was so crazy? I honestly was still hoping for a turnaround to take place, but it just did not happen. My lifelong dream of being married with children, a big house, and the white picket fence was destroyed, and I had no other choice but to trust God to see me through a nasty "no fault divorce." It was not nasty because we were fighting over legal matters or dividing up belongings because we had nothing to fight over, for all we had was each other. It was a nasty to me because it was not what I wanted to take place in my life.

**Unlocking God's Favor,
Single, Married, Divorced,
Remarried**

Remarried

Going through the divorce was a very trying time for me, but after moving back home (we were living out of state) I praise God for my daddy (who is now in heaven). My daddy told me something that has stuck with me, and will be with me for the rest of my life, and that was "If a man wants you, he will let the whole world know it." I found it to be very true. You may ask me, how do I know? I found out after meeting Dr. Percelle George Gregory, who is my Man of God's name, I thought things would be "on and poppin(g)" like the younger say, but I had to wait on God for another five years that seemed like the longest five years of my life.

After all, the Bible does say, "He that findeth a wife findeth a good thing and obtains FAVOR with the Lord." So I made the decision to focus and keep myself busy working with the church, praying, studying the Bible and getting closer to the Lord. This plan worked the best for me. Because while working in the church we were planning the church's annual Holiday Extravaganza and this particular year they decided to add a fashion show component and use the church members for the models. And take a guess who volunteered to be one of the models; that's right, yours truly.

Unlocking God's Favor, Single, Married, Divorced, Remarried

One of my sister's friends from Washington, DC was a close friend with Percelle, who was a fashion coordinator and had other professional businesses. So, after getting the okay from the Pastors they brought him on. There was a rehearsal scheduled for the fashion show, and I was on my way into the sanctuary where we were to rehearse and as I was entering the room Percelle was coming out and we literary ran into each other. I have to tell you, I spoke to him once over the phone prior to his coming to Minnesota but once I saw him, I fell in love with him at first sight. I am so very serious. I promise you, I would have married him on that night.

It was never a desire of mine to have to get a divorce and then remarry because the church I attended taught against divorce and remarriage; it was a part of the doctrine/bylaws based on Matthew 5:32, "But I tell you that anyone who divorces his wife, except for marital unfaithfulness, causes her to become an adulteress, and anyone who marries the divorced woman commits adultery." But due to infidelity that took place in the marriage, I was cleared by God to get a divorce (even though he divorced me). Therefore, I was in good standing to get remarried. I am so glad God knows what and who is best for us. Our pastors, who were not our pastors then, Drs. Rufus Edward, Sr. and Diane Thibodeaux counseled us and later performed the ceremony. We are so grateful they are our pastors and love them dearly.

**Unlocking God's Favor,
Single, Married, Divorced,
Remarried**

When you trust God, more than what you expect will always come to pass because, like it says in Ephesians 3:20, "Now unto him that is able to do exceeding abundantly above all that we ask or think, according to the power that worketh in us;" the power He is referring to, is His word. I have experienced this act of God's power so many times and each time it encourages me to keep moving forward.

It does pay to wait on the Lord and be of good courage. Even though it may have taken five years, it was well worth the wait. We have been together, as of 2015, 31 years and married 26 years and counting.

After being married only 8 1/2 years the first time, I never dreamt of celebrating 26 years of marriage. God Is Faithful and "Won't He Do It?"

Unlocking God's Favor, Single, Married, Divorced, Remarried

In the scripture references, I have listed scriptures for guidance in all four categories, Single, Married, Divorce, and Remarried. I encourage you to get spiritual counseling while seeking a mate and pre-marital counseling if you are planning to get married. What I have shared with you is just a brief synopsis of Single, Married, Divorce, and Remarried. It is well worth your time to get spiritual guidance to help you to make decisions so you can live a life with fewer regrets. I did not the first go round, but the second time around was the greatest thing I could have ever done. You do not have to rush love because real love lasts a lifetime.

Scripture References:
Desiring a mate while SINGLE...

II Corinthians 6:14 (KJV), Be ye not unequally yoked together with unbelievers; for what fellowship hath righteousness with unrighteousness? And what communion hath light with darkness.

Matthew 7:7 (KJV), Ask, and it shall be given you; seek, and ye shall find; knock, and it shall be opened unto you

Mark 11:24 (KJV), Therefore I say unto you, What things soever ye desire, when ye pray, believe that ye receive [them], and ye shall have [them].

**Unlocking God's Favor,
Single, Married, Divorced,
Remarried**

**Scripture References:
Considering MARRIAGE...**

Matthew 7:7 (KJV), Ask, and it shall be given you; seek, and ye shall find; knock and it shall be opened unto you:

Psalms 37:4 (KJV), Delight thyself also in the LORD; and he shall give thee the desires of thine heart.

Proverbs 18:22 (KJV), [Whoso] findeth a wife findeth a good [thing], and obtaineth favour of the LORD.

Mark 11:24 (KJV), Therefore I say unto you, What things so ever ye desire, when ye pray, believe that ye receive [them], and ye shall have [them].

Genesis 2:18 (KJV), And the LORD God said, [It is] not good that the man should be alone; I will make him an help meet for him.

Unlocking God's Favor, Single, Married, Divorced, Remarried

Scripture References: Contemplating DIVORCE...

I Corinthians 7: 15 (NKJV), But if the unbeliever departs, let him depart; a brother or sister is not under bondage in such cases. But God has called us to peace.

I Corinthians 7:16-17 (NKJV), For how do you know, O wife, whether you will save your husband? Or how do you know, O man, whether you will save your wife? But as God has distributed to each one, as the Lord has called each one, so let him walk.

Matthew 19: 6-8 (NKJV), So they are no longer two, but one. Therefore what God has joined together, let man not separate. Why then, they asked, did Moses command that a man give his wife a certificate of divorce and send her away? He said to them "Moses, because of the hardness of their hearts, permitted you to divorce your wives, but from the beginning it as not so."

Unlocking God's Favor, Single, Married, Divorced, Remarried

**Scripture References:
REMARRIED after divorce...**

Philippians 4:19 (NKJV), And my God shall supply all of my need according to His riches in glory by Christ Jesus.

Proverbs 3:5-6 (KJV), Trust in the Lord with all thine heart; and lean not unto thy own understanding. In all they way acknowledge him, and he shall direct your paths.

Psalms 121:1-8 (KJV), I will lift up mine eyes unto the hills, from whence cometh my help. My help cometh from the LORD, which made heaven and earth. He will not suffer thy foot to be moved: he that keepeth thee will not slumber. Behold, he that keepeth Israel shall neither slumber nor sleep. The LORD is thy keeper: the LORD is thy shade upon thy right hand. The sun shall not smite thee by day, nor the moon by night. The LORD shall preserve thee from all evil: he shall preserve thy soul. The LORD shall preserve thy going out and thy coming in from this time forth, and even for evermore.

Chapter VIII
Unlocking God's Favor
For Your Finances

Unlocking God's Favor for Your Finances as far as I am concerned and according to the word of God it is done in only one way and that is through tithing found in Malachi 3:9-11.

My husband and I believe in tithing and stand on this scripture verse, so tough, until the word "TITHE" is displayed on our automobile. The verse on tithing breaks down what happens when one chooses to or chooses not to tithe. If you decide not to tithe it ties God's hands from allowing you to receive what you are in need of, for example, a healthy life including wealth.

In Malachi 3:11 it states, He will rebuke the devourer (pests) for your sake. This means He will stop Satan, the devil himself from robbing you in many ways, including your health, wealth, and prosperity.

**Unlocking God's Favor
For Your Finances**

Through tithing, we have seen God literally change our lifestyle. We have received monies back from the IRS when we were in the process of still owing them. We have been healed on the way to the emergency room, therefore not having to go. Appliances miraculously started working when we had scheduled a service person to come. Consequently, we were able to cancel the service person and thereby, saving us loads of money. Those are examples of rebuking the devourer.

This is not a long chapter, but I wanted to speak on it because I want everyone to know that it pays to follow Jesus. If you obey God and give Him your tithe (10%), He will give you His 90 % and more. Like I quoted earlier from Ephesians 3:20, Now, unto him that is able to do exceeding abundantly above all we can ask or think according to the power that worketh in us. Tithe, and watch God perform His word and keep His promise.

**Unlocking God's Favor
For Your Finances**

**Scripture References:
Finances**

2 Corinthians 9:7, Every man according as he purposeth in his heart, so let him give; not grudgingly, or of necessity: for God loveth a cheerful giver. Luke 6:38, Give and it shall be given unto you; good measure, pressed down, and shaken together, and running over, shall men give into your bosom. For with the same measure that we mete withal it shall be measured to you again.

James 1:17, Every good gift and every perfect gift is from above, and cometh down from the Father of lights with whom is no variableness, neither shadow of turning. Philippians 4:19, But my God shall supply all your need according to his riches in glory by Christ Jesus.

Proverbs 13:22, A good man leaveth an inheritance to his children's children and the wealth of the sinner is laid up for the just.

Proverbs 3:9-10, Honor the Lord with thy substance, and with the first fruits of all thine increase. So shall thy barns be filled with plenty, and thy presses shall burst out with new wine.

**Unlocking God's Favor
For Your Finances**

**Scripture References:
Giving**

Acts 20:35, I have shewed you all things, how that so labouring ye ought to support the weak, and to remember the words of the Lord Jesus, how he said, It is more blessed to give than to receive.

Deuteronomy 15:10, Thou shalt surely give him, and thine heart shall not be grieved when thou givest unto him: because that for this thing the LORD thy God shall bless thee in all thy works, and in all that thou puttest thine hand unto.

Proverbs 22:9, He that hath a bountiful eye shall be blessed; for he giveth of his bread to the poor.

John 3:16, For God so loved the world, that he gave his only begotten Son, that whosoever believeth in him should not perish, but have everlasting life.

2 Corinthians 9:10, Now he that minister seed to the sower both minister bread for your food, and multiply your seed sown, and increase the fruits of your righteousness;).

Psalms 50:14, Offer unto God thanksgiving; and pay thy vows unto the most High:

CHAPTER IX
Unlocking God's Favor
Concerning Salvation

I would like to share with you the most precious gift that you can ever receive in life, and that is the gift of salvation that only comes from Jesus Christ.

Since I have given my life totally and completely over to the Lord Jesus Christ, I have peace that is unexplainable. I feel His love leading and guiding me every day.

If you have not given your heart to the Lord, and you feel this book has given you reason to want to do so, please go to St. John 10:10 and find out why Jesus did, what he did for us; "The thief cometh not, but for to steal, and to kill, and to destroy: I am come that they may have life and have it more abundantly."

You may ask, so, how do I gain this salvation you are speaking about?

**Unlocking God's Favor
Concerning Salvation**

Good question and here is the simple answer that is found in Roman 9:10 "Confess with your mouth the Lord Jesus and believe in your heart that God has raised Him from the dead and thou shall be saved."

Beloved, it is just that easy. Once you give Jesus your heart, you too will be able to unlock His favor on earth as it is in heaven.

After giving your life to Jesus, if you are excited as I was, and I believe you will be, and then you too will begin sharing with others how great it is *Unlocking God's Favor*!
©2015

Food For Thought

Remember when you study the Word, and understand how it works to unlock God's favor, you will then know there are many promises you can gain from having this favor. God's favor can and will cause you to have the favor that is needed on a daily basis. Agree?

God's favor will keep you on top of your game as long as you put Him first. By staying in His perfect will, you will experience the true meaning of...

"The Sky is the Limit."

Contacts
To obtain your copy of
Unlocking God's Favor (Book)
God Has Been Good to Me (CD)
Kingdom Jewels (Jewelry Line)
Visit the online Bookstore
www.bernicegregory.com or bernicegregory54@msn.com

For Bookings
Dr. Percelle G. Gregory
(612) 839-6295 or (612) 325-1407
percellegregory@aol.com
Facebook "Bernice Gregory" or "Percelle Gregory"

Unlocking God's Favor
After reading *UNLOCKING GOD'S FAVOR*, you will be encouraged to go after your lifelong dreams, and live life to its fullest.

This book will give you the opportunity to learn scriptures that you can apply to your everyday life and watch them unfold before your very own eyes. I am not speaking from what I heard, but from what I know and have now experienced.

International Recording Artist and Author
Bernice Brown Gregory

Unlocking God's Favor

About The Author

A native of Minneapolis, Minnesota born and raised on the north side of the city, I was fortunate to be raised by both parents along with five other siblings and a sister in New Orleans.

Growing up we had hard times like most people around us but my parents taught us how to appreciate what we did have and be the best whatever we decided to do and be in life. I always desired to be a singer, but a recording artist was not on the list, that slipped up on me at a later date in life. I must say what really is amazing to me is becoming an author and sharing my life with others in book form. I have been blessed to have had many wonderful things happen to me, and a few of those special things are: a) My moment in my life of accepting Lord Jesus Christ as my Savior and accepting the call to be an ordained minister; b) Becoming wife to Dr. Percelle Gregory; c) A chance to raise my son, James and becoming a grandmother to James Jr., Marcus, many step grandchildren, and a godmother/god-grandmother to many.

Life has a way of shifting in many directions, and becoming an author is one of those unexpected shifts. Below I have also added my music bio for booking purposes and to give you little more insight as to who I am, and who I represent when it comes to my music ministry God has gifted to me. It is my desire, that you and everyone who reads *Unlocking God's Favor* will be blessed and know that it was a pleasure and a delight passing on the information God gave me to share with you of how to unlock His favor.

Blessings and much more!
Bernice Brown Gregory
Minister, Author and International Recording Artist

About the Author Bio

Bernice has been singled out, called upon and chosen by God to speak His word through song to the nations (Psalms 108). God has given Bernice a ministry of exhortation, encouragement and the ability to meet people where they are and lead them to Christ. Bernice is a worshiper of God, and it resonates not only in her music but also in her lifestyle.

Bernice has been singing since the age of nine. Her singing abilities were discovered by her junior high school music instructor, the late Mrs. Jean Norling and gospel music mentor, Evangelist Elgene Meadows.

Over the past several years, Bernice has matured in the natural and spiritual. The Lord's call on her life has taken her gift of song and songwriting to a higher level. She has ministered overseas several times at the Lord's Chapel in Jamaica, and her CD project was featured at the Jubilee Christian Center in London, England. She has also sung with the Benny Hinn Ministries Crusade Choir, Dr. Cindy Trimm's Prayer Tour, and Juanita Bynum Ministries Revival Tour. She has appeared on stage for the Juneteenth Celebrations, Minnesota Soul Liberation Summer Festivals and the Minneapolis Upfront Theater (Tsunami Relief).

She has participated in several workshops. Featured in the Bobby Jones New Artist Show Case in Hollywood, Florida and positioned to share a lead vocal on stage with the Queen of Gospel, Pastor Shirley Caesar. She was featured in and given a leading role in the stage play "Love Covers" written and directed by Dr. Dorie McKnight.

About the Author Bio

Bernice has appeared on the same stages with such renowned artists as Larnelle Harris, Kim Burrell, Micah Stampley, Byron Cage, Richard Smallwood, Martha Munizzi, Shirley Murdock, Tye Tribbett, Helen Baylor, Be Be and CeCe Winans, Yolanda Adams, Clark Sisters, Vanessa Bell Armstrong, the late Thomas Whitfield, Timothy Wright and the three time Grammy Award Winners Sounds of Blackness whom she opened for at the Mall of America in Bloomington, Minnesota. Also, a featured cast member in their "The Night Before Christmas Musical Production (thank you Gary Hines) at the Fitzgerald Theater" St. Paul, Minnesota. Also featured in the Actors For Christ Production (thank you Joyce Marrie). In past times, she has sung with local artist Stellar Award Winners James Grear & Company, Grammy Nominated Excelsior Choral Ensemble, and Roosevelt George. Bernice has done live music for local television programs, hair commercial, and several music videos.

In 2005, Bernice recorded her first debut music CD titled *God's Been Good to Me.*

Having experienced some difficulties in life, Bernice has learned to be grateful. She has seen how her experiences allowed God to take a mess and turn it into a message to win the lost for Christ. Her music not only captivates her audiences but blesses and overwhelms them with compassion, healing and love.

Bernice is humbled and honored God has chosen her to touch the lives of so many people who are hurting, sick, lonely, looking for answers and change. Her songs are both full of hope, healing, encouragement, joy, peace and love.

CPSIA information can be obtained
at www.ICGtesting.com
Printed in the USA
LVOW01s1205290116

472238LV00006B/37/P